The Nativity Story

Written by Sasha Morton
Illustrated by Alfredo Belli

Long ago, in Nazareth, an angel appeared
to a young woman called Mary.

The angel Gabriel spoke to her, and he said:
"You have been chosen by God to
do an important job. You are
going to have his son."

2

Mary told her husband Joseph, who was a good and
kind man. They were both happy to do what God wanted
and looked forward to the arrival of this special child.

Shortly before the baby was due to be born,
Mary and Joseph had to travel to Bethlehem.
Mary trusted that God would look after them
on their travels and she was right.

Still, it was a hard journey and after
several days, they were relieved
to see the town of Bethlehem
before them.

But once they arrived safely in Bethlehem,
they had another problem to face...

5

There was not a single room in the town for them to sleep in.

Poor Mary and Joseph went from one side of Bethlehem to the other, but all they heard were the words, "Sorry, there is no room at the inn."

To make things worse,
Mary realised that the
baby was going to come
very soon. What were
they going to do?

7

Tired and hungry, Mary and Joseph trudged to the very last inn in Bethlehem. Yet again, it was full. However, this particular innkeeper took pity on the young couple who stood before him.

8

"You are welcome to stay in my stable,"
offered the innkeeper. "My animals
are in there too, but it's warm and dry."

9

On that very night, God's Son came into the world.

In the moment he was born, a star,
brighter than any other in the night sky,
began to sparkle over the stable.

The happy parents wrapped Jesus in swaddling cloths, and he slept peacefully on a bed of straw in a manger.

At the same time on a nearby hillside, some shepherds were tending to their sheep. Suddenly, a bright light appeared and an angel stood before them!

"I bring good news," said the angel. "Today in Bethlehem, a baby has been born who is the Son of God. Follow the star and you will find him."

Then, just as quickly as the light had come, it faded. The shepherds looked up in disbelief, and there they saw…

…a dazzling, bright star!

Straight away, the shepherds headed towards the star and soon they arrived at the stable. They crept in and whispered, "An angel told us that the Son of God was here."

Mary and Joseph welcomed the shepherds and showed them their precious child.

The shepherds knelt before
the manger to look at
the baby Jesus.

Not a creature stirred.
All was peaceful.
All was quiet.

15

In the East, unknown to Mary and Joseph,
three wise men had noticed this new bright star.
They studied the word of God and knew it could
only mean one thing – the King of the Jews,
who would save the world, had been born!

One dusky evening, the wise men began their
own journey. The same star guided
them night after night...

through deserted streets…

over miles of dark desert…

...until they found Mary,
Joseph and Jesus.

19

Mary and Joseph were happy to welcome these unexpected visitors who had travelled so far to see God's Son.

The three wise men brought
gifts of gold, frankincense
and myrrh with them.

They were gifts fit for a King.

The birth of Jesus was a miracle,
and soon everyone would know of it.

But on that first night in Bethlehem, in a simple stable, the Son of God slept peacefully on a bed of straw, watched over by those who loved him.

It was the very first Christmas Day.

An Hachette UK Company
www.hachette.co.uk

First published in Great Britain in 2013 by TickTock,
an imprint of Octopus Publishing Group Ltd,
Endeavour House,
189 Shaftesbury Avenue,
London WC2H 8JY.

www.octopusbooks.co.uk

ISBN 978 1 84898 815 6

A CIP record of this book is available from the British Library

Printed and bound in China

1 3 5 7 10 8 6 4 2

With thanks to: Jana Burson

Series Editor: Lucy Cuthew   Design: Advocate Art
Publisher: Tim Cook   Managing Editor: Karen Rigden
Production: Lucy Carter